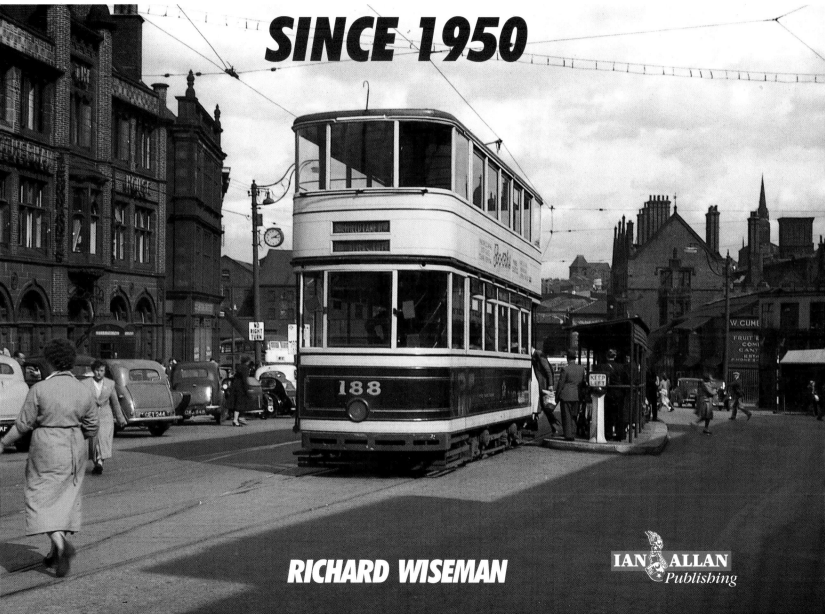

# SHEFFIELD TRAMS IN COLOUR SINCE 1950

**RICHARD WISEMAN**

IAN ALLAN Publishing

First published 1997

ISBN 0 7110 2535 5

Published by Ian Allan Publishing

an imprint of Ian Allan Ltd, Terminal House, Station Approach, Shepperton, Surrey TW17 8AS.
Printed by Ian Allan Printing Ltd at its works at Coombelands in Runnymede, England.

Code: 9709/B3

# Introduction

The city of Sheffield lying on the eastern flanks of the Pennine hills is well known for the high quality of its steel and cutlery products. It was also famous for the high quality of its electric tramway system which served its citizens for over half a century.

The city had expanded along the flat flood-plain of the River Don and the earliest tramway, using horse traction, was opened in 1873 along the valley floor to Tinsley and later to Brightside. These were followed by lines to Hillsborough and Nether Edge. The suburbs developing in the hillier country beyond the valleys had to await the introduction of electric traction over 25 years later.

The first electric tramcars, under corporation ownership, ran from the city centre to Nether Edge and to Tinsley on 5 September 1899. The system rapidly expanded and by 1905 the greater part of the city and its suburbs was served by electric tramcars. However, the tramway system did not stagnate at the then boundaries of the built-up area and extensions continued to be made. The most notable were the reserved tracks along Abbey Lane linking Woodseats with Millhouses via Beauchief, which opened in 1927; and Prince of Wales Road, linking Intake, Elm Tree, with Darnall, which opened in 1928. Unfortunately, lines to serve the new estates then being developed in the hilly country between the Owlerton and Firth Park routes never materialised. Further extensions were opened in the mid-1930s; the last, to Intake (Birley Vale), on 29 December 1935. It had been intended to extend the Meadowhead and Wadsley Bridge routes, but the outbreak of war intervened and the tracks were never laid.

The topography of the Sheffield area covers the flat valley floors extending northeast along the Don valley towards Rotherham, northwest to Hillsborough and Owlerton, and southwest along the Sheaf valley through Abbeydale to Millhouses. The valleys are flanked by hilly country with the steepest sections southeast up City Road to Elm Tree, southwest to Ecclesall and Fulwood, westwards to Crookes, and north to Pitsmoor and Sheffield Lane Top.

The net result was that the city's tramcars were always of the single-truck type and initially only single-deck cars were allowed on the steepest sections, including the 1 in 11 up City Road. However, the development of more powerful motors and improved braking systems allowed double-deck cars to be used, first to Crookes in 1904 and subsequently on the other routes in the next decade.

Another feature of the Sheffield system were the numerous sharp bends, especially on the Crookes route which could boast five (although one was initially a junction at the top of Witham Road). It should be noted that the majority of Sheffield's tramcars were equipped with four braking systems: air-operated track and wheel brakes used for service stops, magnetic track brakes for emergency stops plus the standard wheel and track handbrakes used mainly for parking.

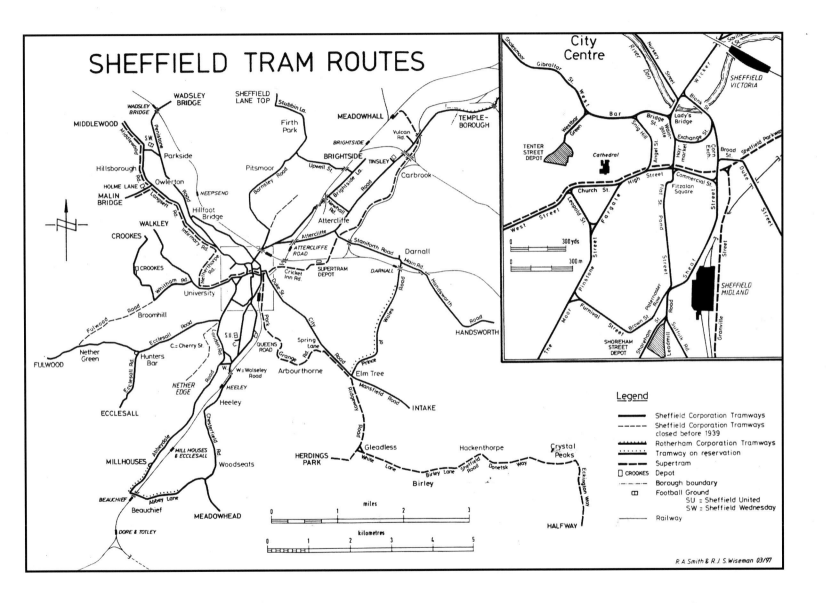

# SHEFFIELD TRAM ROUTES

**City Centre**

Legend
- Sheffield Corporation Tramways
- Sheffield Corporation Tramways closed before 1939
- Rotherham Corporation Tramways
- Tramway on reservation
- Supertram
- CROOKES  Depot
- Borough boundary
- Football Ground
  SU = Sheffield United
  SW = Sheffield Wednesday
- Railway

R.A.Smith & R.J.S.Wiseman 03/97

The city streets have witnessed the development of the electric tramcar from its initial uncanopied, open-top state of 1899, through the addition of top covers and vestibules to the all-enclosed, less angular and very comfortable 'Jubilee' car of 1946. This sequence was due to the progressive policy of replacing rather than rebuilding the city's tramcars from 1918 onwards, and as a result, by 1936 all of the original fleet had been replaced by new vehicles with the exception of the 15 'Preston' cars of 1907. These were scheduled to be replaced in 1939-40, but by that time wartime conditions and increasing traffic required every available tramcar to be in service. Further cars were obtained second-hand from Bradford and Newcastle in 1941 and 1943 respectively.

The replacement policy was initially continued after the war with the building of the 'Jubilee' car No 501 in Queen's Road works and the purchase of 35 similar cars from Charles Roberts of Horbury. These were delivered in 1950-2 and proved to be the last new cars; from then on the trams were replaced by diesel buses, although some of the 'Standard' cars continued to be improved. Today, after a gap of 35 years, the High Street is once again served by tramcars, the modern single-deck Supertrams.

The apogee of the Sheffield tramcar is not so easy to define. Was it in the period 1936-9 when new cars predominated, when the tracks, mainly paved in asphalt, were in first-class condition and fares were cheap? Others might say it was during the wartime years when factories were working a three-shift system and other means of local transport were very limited; or was it in the immediate postwar years, say 1947 to 1952, when wartime difficulties and shortages had been overcome, maintenance was back to its prewar best and the motorcar had yet to make its impact on the city streets?

I have to accept the latter choice if only for the reason that this was the period when I came to know the Sheffield tramway system and also because few colour photographs were taken prior to that date. My own photographs date from 1957, but fortunately I have been able to draw on other sources. Even so, it has not been possible to cover all the system as it existed before the abandonment programme began in 1952 with the withdrawal of the Hunter's Bar to Fulwood section and the line from Holme Lane depot to Malin Bridge. This was followed by Ecclesall-Middlewood in 1954 with further closures taking place until the final trams ran from Beauchief to Vulcan Road on 1 October 1960.

As Sheffield is fortunate in having a new tramway it seems logical to show the system through the development of its tramcars as indicated above. Thus we start with the 'Preston' and 'Rocker Panel' cars and continue through the more modern vehicles up to the 'Roberts' cars of 1950. We then look briefly at the demise of the original system, followed by the preservation era, before a grand finale with trams once again gracing the city centre streets.

R. J. S. Wiseman
Barton
May 1997

# Acknowledgements

I would like to thank Roy Brook, C. Carter and Jim Copland for allowing me to use their photographs in this book. As a result of their help it has been possible to add to the variety of locations depicted. A map of the Sheffield tramway systems has been included and for this I thank Roger Smith for undertaking the task. I also wish to record my thanks to Charles Hall for information on Sheffield's tramways over the years, and to my wife for help throughout the compilation of the book.

Books and periodicals consulted include *Sheffield Corporation Tramways* by Robert Gandy and various issues of *Modern Tramway* and *Tramway Review*.

*Left:*
Trams have returned to Sheffield with the present-day Supertram. The Cathedral station, opposite the Cutlers Hall, is well placed for the shops in Fargate but is some distance from The Moor. No 09 has reversed here and is about to start its journey to Herdings Park on 26 August 1996. *R. J. S. Wiseman.*

# The 'Preston' Cars

Built in 1907 by United Electric Car Co at Preston as balcony cars, they were initially numbered 258-272. No 259 was fitted with upper-deck vestibules in 1911 as an experiment; the rest were fitted with new vestibuled upper decks between December 1924 and July 1927. Renumbred 336-350, they were scheduled for scrapping in 1939, but due to war conditions 11 cars were retained and the last, No 339, was not scrapped until 8 February 1957.

'Preston' No 346 is seen at the final Intake terminus at the then Derbyshire boundary. It was photographed on the occasion of a special tour of the system on 1 May 1955. These cars were not fitted with airbrakes and were banned from the 1 in 9½ gradient of Duke Street. Intake terminus could only be reached via Prince of Wales Road and Elm Tree. *Roy Brook*

*Left:*
The Crookes route, however, involved a circuitous climb of over 350ft and with its easier gradients was therefore accessible to the 'Preston' cars. No 346 is at the terminus and beyond can be glimpsed the valley along which the Supertram now runs to Malin Bridge and Middlewood. *Jim Copland*

*Above:*
The 'Preston' tour started at 1pm outside the Midland station for Meadowhead, Abbey Lane, Millhouses and Owlerton. Some two hours later No 346 reached Tinsley depot where, thanks to the co-operation of the staff, this line-up of three 'Prestons' — Nos 346, 342 and 339 — with No 474, a 'Rocker Panel' car, in the background, was drawn up. No 342 was later preserved.

Part of the depot now houses the Sheffield Bus Museum in which the lower deck of No 460 is currently being restored. *Jim Copland*

*Left:*
A busy scene in Pond Street before the new technical college was built, with the driver of No 49 waiting patiently for passengers to board and alight. Note the elaborate lining-out in gold, a reminder of the days when cities were proud of their trams. The date is 19 September 1950. *C. Carter*

*Below*
There were two sections of single line on the route to Wadsley Bridge which followed the Don valley and was one of the first areas to be industrially developed. No 42, a Brush car of 1924 and one of the last to be scrapped in 1957, is seen entering the first section in Nursery Street in 1954. There has been considerable redevelopment in the area subsequently. *Roy Brook*

# The 'Rocker Panel' Cars

The prototype car, No 366, was built at Queens Road works in 1917 and was followed by three others by 1921 (Nos 367-9). The production cars, however, were built by outside contractors between 1919 and 1927: Nos 376-450 and Nos 36-60 by Brush at Loughborough, and Nos 451-500 by Cravens at Darnall, Sheffield. Fitted with wooden seats originally, the majority were later provided with leather upholstered seats.

*Left:*
No 42 is seen at Fitzalan Square on a sunny day in September 1955, *en route* from Woodseats to Wadsley Bridge. At the far side of the square is the High Street/Haymarket intersection — the hub of the system. *Jim Copland*

*Above:*
On 22 May 1956 No 42 was photographed rounding the corner from Barnsley Road to Stubbin Lane on its way down to Firth Park and the city centre. The only change here over the past 40 years is the increase in traffic. *Jim Copland*

# The 'Standard' Cars

These date from 1927 when the prototype car No 1, built by Cravens, entered service. It was the first of a series of straight-sided cars — Nos 2-35, 61-130, 156-230 and 243-248 were built at the Queens Road works, and a further 25, Nos 131-155, were built by W. E. Hill & Sons of South Shields. A new livery of cream with blue bands was introduced with No 202 in 1935, and, starting with No 87 in 1952, 23 cars had their lower saloons rebuilt during the next two years.

*Above:*
The prototype, No 1, was built by Cravens at Darnall and entered service in December 1927. It is seen at Wadsley Bridge terminus on the occasion of a special tour on 29 April 1956. The extension of the tram route to the city boundary was to have been in the centre reservation of a dual-carriageway road. This was later constructed without the tramway. *Roy Brook*

*Above:*
Flat Street was the city terminus for services to Woodseats via Queens Road or Shoreham Street and for Intake via City Road which were routed via Sheaf Street. No 113, however, will reverse on the crossover and load at Fitzalan Square for Darnall, Prince of Wales Road and Elm Tree. The crowd in the background is probably waiting for trams to the Wednesday football ground at Hillsborough. *Roy Brook*

*Right:*
Tramcars on the Handsworth-Crookes service turned left into Blonk Street and then continued to the Corn Exchange before turning right into Commercial Street. No 179 was photographed in Blonk Street on 22 May 1956. This view is taken from the bridge over the River Don looking south towards the Sheffield canal basin, which has since been renovated and is now a heritage site. The Samuel Osborne steelworks, where tram track was manufactured, can be seen on the left side of the road (now a dual-carriageway and part of the inner ring road). *Jim Copland*

*Above:*
No 123 was repainted in the newer livery in the 1950s and is seen standing on the through line from Pinstone Street at the Leopold Street/Fargate junction. No 123 will continue down Fargate as the Leopold Street tracks were mainly used for reversing cars from the north and east. Note the loading refuge, the quality stop sign with its polished wood surround which would have shown Middlewood at an earlier date, and the pedestrian crossing linking the stop to the pavement. *Jim Copland*

*Right:*
Handsworth terminus is the setting for this view of No 159. Originally in the dark blue livery, this car was repainted in the cream livery in 1945 after its wartime grey. *Roy Brook*

*Right:*
As mentioned earlier, a number of 'Standard' cars had their lower saloon rebuilt in the 1950s. The major visible change was the elimination of the ventilation lights above the lower saloon windows as seen in this view of No 161 at Sheffield Lane Top, taken on 22 May 1956. No 217 to the rear is in original condition, as built in 1935. The public house is another of the amenities serving the locals. *Jim Copland*

*Above:*
At the terminus, in May 1956, the driver of No 215 starts on the return journey to the city and demonstrates the trolley reverser with the pole at full stretch. *Jim Copland*

*Right:*
Sheffield Lane Top was the nearest the trams got to serving Shiregreen, one of the large new housing estates built during the interwar years. No 177 is standing at the terminus and awaiting passengers before setting off on the return journey to Woodseats and Abbey Lane in May 1956. *Jim Copland*

18

*Left:*
No 115 was another of the cars to have its lower saloon rebuilt and it is seen here in September 1960 waiting to use the Millhouses crossover in the last few months of operation when the turning circle was being converted for bus use. *R. J. S. Wiseman*

*Above:*
The Millhouses route was extended on reserved track to Beauchief in 1927. It followed the Sheaf valley, as the railway still does, and on an October afternoon in 1957 the sun glints on No 206 and the birches of Ecclesall woods which cover the hillside to the left. The site of the tram tracks has since been incorporated into the road. *R. J. S. Wiseman*

*Above:*
At Beauchief there was a sharp turn left into Abbey Lane. On a sunny day in the spring of 1957, No 194 is waiting for the traffic signal to give a green light before turning the corner. The Sheaf valley was the scene of early industrial development and it was only a short walk from the tram stop to the Abbeydale industrial complex.
*R. J. S. Wiseman*

*Right:*
Coming into Abbey Lane there was a gradual climb to cross the Midland main line at Beauchief station which closed some months before the tram service. Despite its imminent conversion, the tram was given as one of the alternative services. The last remnants of the autumn sunshine glint on No 190 as it pulls away from the tram stop, a cast-metal plate, in October 1957.
*R. J. S. Wiseman*

*Above:*
Beyond the bridge the tracks veer to the north side on to a grassed reservation and we reach the site of Beauchief Abbey, off the picture to the left, where No 221 is on its way down to Beauchief. The golf course lies to the left with the Derbyshire hills beyond. My wife and elder son are to be seen on the bench, tram spotting. Both our sons developed a lifelong interest in, and subsequent careers connected with, transport. *R. J. S. Wiseman*

*Right:*
Continuing up the hill we reach Folds Crescent, which No 160 has just passed on its way up to Woodseats on an autumn day in 1957. The curving nature of the line can be appreciated from this point. *R. J. S. Wiseman*

*Above:*
Towards Woodseats the tracks were located in the carriageway and on a damp Monday morning on 20 January 1958 an almost empty No 226 leaves the compulsory stop, marked by the two white rings on the lamp post, at Abbey Lane cemetery. On the Abbey Lane and Prince of Wales Road circles the stops showed 'up cars' and 'down cars' depending on the direction of travel. *R. J. S. Wiseman*

*Right:*
Meadowhead was an extension of the Woodseats route and involved a 1 in 11 gradient. It served Graves Park and new housing development at Norton. The terminus was a short distance south of the park entrance where No 23 is waiting to depart for Sheffield Lane Top on 17 March 1957. This was the author's first colour photograph of a tram. *R. J. S. Wiseman*

26

*Above:*
Back to Millhouses and happy days in 1956! 8 August was a beautiful day and
Millhouses Park was crowded. The park's facilities included a swimming pool,
sports pitches and other amenities. No 199 would be one of a number of cars
running a shuttle service to the city taking the crowds home. *Jim Copland*

# 'Domed-roof' Class

These cars mark the final phase in the development of the standard Sheffield tramcar. Introduced in 1936, Nos 231-242 and Nos 249-303 were all built at Queens Road works, the last entering service in March 1939. In addition, a further 14 were later built to replace cars lost by enemy action during World War 2. With white-painted ceilings, improved lighting and moquette-upholstered seats, these were very attractive vehicles.

*Above:*
No 268 stands on the track fan at the entrance to Crookes depot on a bright sunny March day in 1957. The depot was opened in 1920. Situated in an elevated position, its snowplough often came in handy as snow tended to stay longer on the hills. One memorable occasion was 17 May 1955 when the plough was needed to keep the tracks clear. Fortunately, at that time of the year, the snow did not last.
*R. J. S. Wiseman*

*Left:*
The Firth Park route also involved a climb or two: up Spital Hill from The Wicker, then down to Firvale before climbing again towards Firth Park. No 258 is passing Abbeyfield Park at the Pitsmoor Toll Bar on 28 February 1960, a little over a month before the route closed. *Jim Copland*

*Below:*
We return again to the two major tramway projects of the 1920s with two wintry scenes. The Hutcliffe Wood Road stop was probably the busiest on Abbey Lane as witnessed by the shelter, the telephone kiosk and the pedestrian crossing. There were also shops and a post office nearby. No 258 is on its way back to Vulcan Road in January 1959. The cup-tie sign was to divert traffic from the south round via Abbeydale Road to Bramall Lane. *R. J. S. Wiseman*

*Right:*
A late spring snowfall in early March 1958 adds a touch of white to the Prince of Wales Road as No 237 moves away from the stop serving the centre of the Manor estate. *R. J. S. Wiseman*

*Above:*
Fourteen trams were destroyed or badly damaged in the Sheffield blitz of December 1940 and replacement bodies were built at Queen's Road for them during 1941-4. No 192 is at Woodseats, approaching the junction at the bottom of Meadowhead on 20 September 1955. Advertisements were introduced on tramcars in 1952 for the first time since the end of 1916. *Jim Copland*

*Right:*
Two of the 'Rocker Panel' cars, Nos 430 and 483, also had to have new bodies. The latter is seen at Millhouses on 26 May 1956, with No 233 behind waiting to go round the loop. *Jim Copland*

*Above:*
Waiting to leave the loop on 26 April 1954 is No 474, with No 263 following on with an extra working through to Sheffield Lane Top. *Roy Brook*

## 'Roberts' Cars

The prototype 'Jubilee' car, No 501, was the last car to be built at the Queens Road works and entered service in August 1946. The series cars were built by Charles Roberts & Co of Horbury, Wakefield, in 1950-2.

*Right:*
A fine portrait of No 532 at Handsworth terminus. When photographed in July 1953 this car was only two years old and was, alas, to be scrapped seven years later. *Roy Brook*

*Above:*
Woodseats terminus viewed shortly before the withdrawal of the Wadsley Bridge service on 3 October 1959 and its replacement by Atlantean buses. No 511 will reverse and return to the city, while people at the new bus stop, with new shelter, wait for the infrequent bus service that replaced the tram service seven months earlier. *Jim Copeland*

*Right:*
Pond Street is the setting for No 503 on its way to Woodseats. The Sheffield Polytechnic was under construction when this car was photographed on 22 May 1956. *Jim Copland*

*Left:*
No 503 on Queens Road approaches the junction with Shoreham Street on its way to Heeley and Woodseats. This was a typical Sheffield street scene with its terraced houses and small shops. The hills in the background are now served by the new tramway built to serve the Park Grange estates. *R. J. S. Wiseman*

*Above:*
Leaving Heeley, Chesterfield Road climbs above the Sheaf valley before gradually descending to Woodseats. One of the high points is at Scarsdale Road where, on 16 February 1958, No 511 is seen heading to the city while No 277 is outbound. The telegraph poles, the symbol of an earlier communications era, are long since gone. *R. J. S. Wiseman*

*Above:*
In 1959 a roundabout was constructed at the Ecclesall Road junction where No 527, *en route* to Meadowhead, is seen on 28 February 1960. There was once a three-way junction here with lines to Nether Edge (abandoned in 1934) via Cemetery Road and to Ecclesall and Fulwood via Hunter's Bar. *Jim Copland*

*Right:*
There was a similar, but much earlier, roundabout at Firth Park. Here No 505 was also photographed early in 1960. In its heyday Firth Park was a very busy intermediate terminus, especially at peak periods when extra cars from Tinsley, Brightside and elsewhere would terminate here. Two crossovers were needed to deal with cars reversing at this point. *R. J. S. Wiseman*

*Left:*
After the abandonment of the direct
Intake route in 1956, the Prince of
Wales Road circular services were
replaced by a service via Darnall which
terminated at Elm Tree. In May 1957
the junctions were replaced by a stub
terminus at the end of the central
reservation on which No 507 is
reversing. There is scope for extending
Supertram from this point to Darnall
and Meadowhall. *R. J. S. Wiseman*

*Right:*
Newhall Road provided a useful link
between Darnall, Attercliffe and
industrial Brightside. After the
withdrawal of the Exchange Street to
Sheffield Lane Top service on
26 October 1957 it was used for depot
runs only. It was finally closed to trams
when the remaining service — part day
only, Fitzalan Square to Brightside via
Savile Street — was withdrawn on
28 February 1957. No 516 was the last
car from Tinsley to take up duty via
this road. *R. J. S. Wiseman*

# Central Sheffield

*Above:*

The main road north from Sheffield centre was across Lady's Bridge and along The Wicker, a wide thoroughfare with ample room for a double-track tramway and, at tram stops, passenger refuges on each side of the tracks. As shown previously, it was intensively used in its heyday and even in 1956 it was still busy. 'Standard' car No 125, working to Fitzalan Square, is followed by No 264, a 'Domed-roof' car from Crookes depot and probably due to turn left into Blonk Street. Note that by this time the Sheffield-Manchester railway line had been electrified. *Jim Copland*

*Right:*

By 1960, however, The Wicker was seeing increased road traffic and fewer tramcars. On the morning of the last day, 8 October 1960, before the rains came, No 506 pursues its lone course towards Attercliffe and the Vulcan Road terminus at Tinsley. *R. J. S. Wiseman*

*Above:*
The Moor is one of the city's major shopping streets, and at Moorhead there was a triangle junction with double tracks on either side of the Crimea Monument leading down Furnival Street to the Midland station. They were used by peak-hour specials from the east end to Ecclesall and Millhouses. No 15 has drawn up at the tram stop in September 1955, The Moor is now pedestrianised and a short section of track and part of the pointwork remains *in situ*, but the Crimea Monument has been removed. *Jim Copland*

*Above:*
Another busy artery was London Road leading south from The Moor through Highfields, a well-populated inner suburb. A variety of shops line the road and parked cars line the pavement. No 503, approaching Abbeydale Road junction in this picture taken around 1960, appears to be holding up a bus and a line of cars, a situation that could have been remedied by providing space at stops for other traffic to pass, as with modern systems. There have been few changes here: F. W. Otto's shop still trades in furniture and 'The Tramcar' inn, although out of sight to the left, still welcomes customers. *R. J. S. Wiseman*

# The Green Livery

*Left:*

Sheffield citizens received a shock in 1952 when a number of trams and buses appeared in a new green livery. Such was the public outcry that it was only applied to 14 'Standard' and nine 'Domed-roof' cars; within two years it had disappeared. There were two colour schemes, overall green or a lighter green relieved by dark green bands. No 202 in the all-over green stands at the final Handsworth terminus by Orgreave Lane on the then main A57 road. This extension opened on 7 September 1934 and the route closed on 4 May 1957. *Roy Brook*

# Permanent Way and Works Cars

In order to provide a first-class service it was necessary to keep the tracks clear and in good condition. For this purpose the corporation kept a fleet of works vehicles. At maximum there were 14 snowploughs and five others, including corrugation car No 371 and breakdown car No 375 which had started life as horse car No 15 of The Sheffield Tramways Co. This car is now restored and on show at Crich. A replacement for No 371 was ex-Bradford No 330, which is also at Crich. The snowploughs were all converted from passenger cars and saw regular use each winter.

*Above:*

The Sheffield tracks were kept in good condition throughout the life of the corporation system, the last major renewal being the pointwork at the junction of Shoreham Street and Suffolk Road overnight on the 14-15 May 1955. Traditional methods were used for day-to-day maintenance and included red flags, stop signs and the trackwork bus. On 18 February 1958 No 236 was photographed at the Woodseats end of Abbey Lane. *R. J. S. Wiseman*

*Above:*
No 359 was converted from Brush open-top car No 111 in March 1924. It was specially brought out of Tinsley depot into the open in September 1959 during one of the regular monthly visits to work on No 189, seen in the background. 'Standard' car No 189 was presented to the Tramway Museum Society shortly before withdrawal of the Prince of Wales Road service. *R. J. S. Wiseman*

*Right:*
No 365 was originally Preston-built No 77 of 1900 and was to converted to a snowplough in January 1929. After 30 years of active service it is being pushed on its last journey, the short distance from the depot to Ward's scrapyard in April 1960. *R. J. S. Wiseman*

*Above:*
The original single-deck cars had five-window saloons, but those converted to snowploughs had one window removed. No 354 was originally Milnes car No 46 built in 1899 and converted in 1920. It stands at the entrance to Tenter Street depot.

The depot, opened in 1928, was the last in operational use. There was a bus depot on the upper level. No 46, another survivor of the Sheffield system, was restored for the final procession and is now at Crich. *R. J. S. Wiseman*

## Odd Events

*Above:*

The first Leyland Atlantean buses in the city replaced the Wadsley Bridge-Woodseats tramcars on 4 October 1959. Their seating capacity was 78 passengers compared with the trams' 61 or 62, and the crews objected to carrying standing passengers as well. The result was a strike from Monday 19 October to Thursday 5 November. However, the trams ran on the first day and No 167 is at the Springfield Road stop on Abbeydale Road, close by Millhouses & Ecclesall station. It would be a long uphill walk to the latter suburb. *R. J. S. Wiseman*

*Left:*
The visit of HM The Queen Mother to Sheffield on 17 May 1958 resulted in the temporary closure of Pinstone Street to tram traffic, and cars from the south were terminated at the Moorhead and reversed on the single line which had been left for such emergencies in Furnival Street. This caused a queue of trams down The Moor as reversing facilities were limited. No 220 awaits its turn to run into Furnival Street.
*R. J. S. Wiseman*

# Specials

*Above:*
Football specials ran to both the Wednesday and United grounds. Those for the Wednesday ground at Hillsborough loaded in Bridge Street and were stacked in Parkside Road. Those for the United ground loaded in Blonk Street and a number were stored in Wolseley Road and the Cherry Street siding, which was adjacent to the ground, for the duration of the match.

On 24 August 1957 Nos 198, 131 and one other are seen stacked in Cherry Street.
*R. J. S. Wiseman*

*Above:*
As in other cities where tramways were being abandoned, special tours were arranged for enthusiasts, usually on the Sunday prior to a route closure. No 102, one of the first cars to be renovated with a rebuilt lower saloon, is seen at Norfolk Bridge, near Attercliffe Road station, on 20 September 1953. *Jim Copland*

*Right:*
The 'Roberts' car tour using No 536 on 22 February 1959 was arranged as a farewell to the Abbey Lane link. It was a bright sunny day and appropriately a stop was made in Abbey Lane, seen here looking east with Chancet Wood as a backdrop. The roses, however, were not in bloom. *R. J. S. Wiseman*

*Left:*
The weather was also fine later in the year, on 27 September, when No 251 was used for a tour which included the Wadsley Bridge route due to close the following Saturday night. The tour used the 'football special' line via Penistone Road to Hillfoot Bridge where the conductor is seen preparing to change the trolley so that the car can be reversed for the return journey to the city. The industrial nature of the Don valley, dominated by the cooling towers of the power station, can be appreciated. *R. J. S. Wiseman*

*Above:*
Three cars were needed for the tour on 27 March 1960 which included visits to Sheffield Lane Top and Meadowhead. 'Roberts' cars Nos 502 and 518 along with No 222 (destined to be the last car from Beauchief six months later) as a back-up, were used. No 502 was later replaced by 'Jubilee' car No 501, Nos 502, 518 and 222 are pictured on Blonk Street. *R. J. S. Wiseman*

# The Last Week

*Left:*
The summer of 1960, although the last for the traditional tramcar in Sheffield, still saw an interesting variety of vehicles on the remaining route which linked Beauchief with Tinsley. It was possible to ride on four types of car: an original 'Standard' dating from 1935, a rebuilt 'Standard', a 'Domed-roof' or a modern 'Roberts' car. By October the fleet had been reduced to 39 cars and three of them were used on the final tour of the system which took place on 2 October 1960. It was a privilege to have the two decorated cars, Nos 510 and 513, together with Jubilee car No 501. The three cars are seen together in Wolseley Road.
*R. J. S. Wiseman*

*Above:*
Beauchief terminus was a pleasant spot at which to watch the trams on a summer's evening. No 523, with 514 behind, was photographed during the last few weeks of operation. The roof lights can be clearly seen from this angle. The crossover from this terminus, together with the shelter, later went to Crich.
*R. J. S. Wiseman*

*Left:*
Services on the last day, Saturday 8 October 1960, were withdrawn during the afternoon, and No 222, working a midday special from Leopold Street to Millhouses, extended on its last journey to Beauchief, was the last public service car. Tinsley depot was reached at about 4pm in pouring rain. The system closed with a procession of 15 cars headed by the illuminated car, No 349, and the two cars destined for Crich, Nos 46 and 189. Nos 513 and 510 completed the procession. This was the scene at Tenter Street depot shortly before the start at 6pm. *Roy Brook*

*Right:*
The original short-canopy Sheffield car was missing from the Crich collection, but again good fortune came to the rescue. In 1922 Sheffield sold 11 cars to Gateshead and the lower saloon of one of these, No 74, was rescued from a Gateshead garden. It was rebuilt at Crich to original condition incorporating materials from the upper decks of cars Nos 215 and 218. It is posed alongside the exhibition hall. *R. J. S. Wiseman*

# Preservation

*Above:*

The tramway preservation movement was fortunate in that Sheffield Corporation was prepared to store tramcars in its Tinsley depot, and that by the time the tramways were being abandoned in Sheffield, Leeds and Glasgow, a site had been found for a museum. It was this good fortune that enabled six Sheffield tramcars to be preserved at Crich and two at Beamish.

Two of the cars, Nos 46 and 189, after completing their final runs in Sheffield at Queen's Road works, were transported to Crich three weeks later, on 28 October 1960. In this view No 189 has already been unloaded, while the crane attends to No 46. It was a typical breezy autumn day with showers and a rainbow. *R. J. S. Wiseman*

*Right:*

No 510, the last traditional tram, was, together with No 513, specially decorated for the final procession to mark the closure of the tramway system on 8 October 1960. No 510 was preserved and has now been longer at Crich (37 years) than it was in service at Sheffield (nine years, 11 months). Standing at the Town End terminus in March 1994 it awaits the signal to proceed down the main line to Glory Mine. Leeds railcar No 602 will then take its place. *R. J. S. Wiseman*

# The Supertram Arrives

Proposals for a new tram system for the South Yorkshire conurbation were first aired in the 1970s, some 12 years after the demise of the original system. A number of routes were examined and eventually two lines were authorised: line 1 from Middlewood, including a branch to Malin Bridge, to Halfway; and line 2 from the delta junction at the bottom of Commercial Street to Meadowhall.

*Above:*
Construction of the new system started in 1992 on line 2 to Meadowhall together with the depot on Woodbourn Road. Work on line 1 followed and the system was completed with installation of the final pointwork at Holme Lane junction at Hillsborough in October 1995. Track laying was mechanised and the concrete is being spread over the steel reinforcement in Middlewood Road on 24 May 1995. *R. J. S. Wiseman*

*Right:*
On the same day another crew were planting poles in Holme Lane. Mother and daughter had just returned from a visit to the nearby shops and stopped to watch the proceedings. *R. J. S. Wiseman*

*Above:*
In November 1994 the contractors were still at work on the Halfway section and used mobile platforms, successors to the tower wagon, for erecting the overhead line on the ballasted sections. They are seen at rest on Sunday 6 November.
*R. J. S. Wiseman*

*Left:*
This view shows the overhead wire being erected in Ridgeway Road on 22 September 1994. *R. J. S. Wiseman*

# The Meadowhall Line

*Left:*
Under the shadow of the M1 viaduct at Tinsley, No 18 speeds off the single line on 10 October 1995. The single line continues round to the left to terminate adjacent to the Meadowhall railway and bus interchange. *R. J. S. Wiseman*

*Above:*
The footbridge over the ex-LNER line to Rotherham and Doncaster gives a good view of Carbrook station with No 05 *en route* to Meadowhall. The railway was reduced to single track to make space for Supertram and a retail park now occupies the site once in industrial use. *R. J. S. Wiseman*

*Above:*
Beyond Attercliffe station the tramway crosses the Sheffield Canal on an elegant
new bridge built to match the footbridge from which the photograph was taken on
4 June 1996. No 22 will no doubt beat the barge to the city centre.

*R. J. S. Wiseman*

## The Halfway Line

*Above:*
During the construction period I would walk back from Halfway and have my lunch at Donetz Way sitting on a convenient stone. The tracks were laid during the summer of 1994 and included a crossover seen in the picture taken on 11 October 1995 with No 19 at speed. *R. J. S. Wiseman*

*Left:*
Trams returned to City Road on 5 December 1994 after a gap of 38 years. No 09 is
in the vicinity of Windy House Lane on the approach to Manor Top (shown as
Intake, Elm Tree on the older trams) on 24 June 1996. *R. J. S. Wiseman*

*Above:*
The initial opening of the line brought the trams up Park Grange Road to the City
Road at Spring Lane station on 22 August 1994. No 18, on a Cathedral-Herdings
Park working, is about to depart after a disabled passenger has alighted. A mother
with buggy is waiting on the opposite platform for a tram to town. The date is
26 August 1996. *R. J. S. Wiseman*

*Left:*
It is a long climb up Park Grange Road and from a footbridge there is a fine panoramic view of the city and its western suburbs, but the Midland main line is hidden from view. No 25 was photographed on 26 August 1996. *R. J. S. Wiseman*

*Above:*
Once at the level of the railway the tramway was built on the alignment of Granville Street. No 06 is departing from the Sheffield station stop for Halfway, also on 26 August 1996. A direct link gives access to main line platforms. *R. J. S. Wiseman*

# City Centre

*Left:*
The hub of the system is the delta junction built over a large roundabout at the bottom of Commercial Street. No 07 is seen on 26 August 1996 on a bank holiday working from Meadowhall to Halfway taking the left-hand curve towards the Midland Station.
*R. J. S. Wiseman*

*Above:*
Initially only the tracks from Cricket Inn Road to Fitzalan Square were in use and No 01 is seen on 26 March 1994, five days after opening. Note that destination blinds were not fitted at this stage, and 'pole 000' in the centre of the junctions. Supertram carried on the tradition of giving poles a location letter as well as a number. *R. J. S. Wiseman*

75

*Left:*
In September 1995 No 08 crosses from Commercial Street to High Street. In the previous era this was a busy tramway junction with trams in all directions, including north-south and east-west services. *R. J. S. Wiseman*

*Above:*
No 24 heads down the High Street towards Fitzalan Square on 19 May 1995. The crossover is provided for trams terminating at the Cathedral until 16 February it was used by the Cathedral-Herdings service which now runs direct from Herdings to Meadowhall, Fargate, out of the picture, is to the right. *R. J. S. Wiseman*

*Left:*
Sheffield Corporation No 222 was one of the cars used on the special tour of 27 March 1960 and was thus routed over tracks not in regular use. It is seen here taking the curve from Leopold Street into Church Street. Note the tarred tracks leading into West Street; these had to be dug up over three decades later and replaced by new ones, albeit on a new alignment. *R. J. S. Wiseman*

*Above:*
No 07 is seen again in the same location on 19 September 1995. The old buildings to the left have been replaced, but those in the background have been cleaned to reveal their Victorian splendour. *R. J. S. Wiseman*

79